This book belongs to

is Amazing

To all of my fans, the Amazies. I want to thank my mom and
RuPaul for inspiring me to be myself, always. —D.N.

To my fabulous and funny, talented and stunning friend who feels
like family, the incredible Lynn Scurfield —D.G.

Farrar Straus Giroux Books for Young Readers
An imprint of Macmillan Publishing Group, LLC
120 Broadway, New York, NY 10271

Text copyright © 2020 by Desmond Napoles
Pictures copyright © 2020 by Dylan Glynn
All rights reserved
Color separations by Bright Arts (H.K.) Ltd.
Printed in China by RR Donnelley Asia Printing Solutions Ltd.,
Dongguan City, Guangdong Province
Designed by Monique Sterling
Art directed by Jen Keenan
First edition, 2020

1 3 5 7 9 10 8 6 4 2

mackids.com

Library of Congress Control Number: 2019948809
ISBN: 978-0-374-31258-9

Our books may be purchased in bulk for promotional, educational, or business use. Please contact your local
bookseller or the Macmillan Corporate and Premium Sales Department at (800) 221-7945 ext. 5442 or by
email at MacmillanSpecialMarkets@macmillan.com.

Be Amazing

A History of Pride

BY **DESMOND IS AMAZING**   PICTURES BY **DYLAN GLYNN**

Farrar Straus Giroux

New York

Hi! My name is Desmond.

I'm a drag kid and LGBTQ advocate. LGBTQ stands for lesbian, gay, bisexual, transgender, and queer.

I live in New York City, where I like to play video games, read, sing, collect toy trains, dance, and model. I enjoy going to school and have many friends.

When I'm not being just Desmond, I like to dress up as characters of a different gender. This is called drag. My drag persona is "Desmond is Amazing."

My motto is: **Be yourself always.**

I can be myself thanks to my parents, who let me be me . . .

. . . and thanks to the very brave
people who fought to make it okay
for me, or anyone like me, to

*be whoever we
want to be.*

I'm lucky because most people accept me for who I am.
In fact, lots of people think I'm pretty *amazing*.

Some people don't, but you know what I always say?

"PAY THE HATERS NO MIND,

THEY'LL NEVER BE AS FIERCE AS YOU AND I."

In the past, it wasn't always possible for people to dress or act or live any way they wanted.

Throughout history, LGBTQ people have been punished,
humiliated, attacked, and discriminated against.

They could lose their jobs, be forced into hospitals, or
even get arrested, just for being who they were.

The Stonewall Inn was one of the few safe spaces for LGBTQ people in New York
City. However, the Stonewall Inn and other places like it were often raided and
shut down by the police as a way to bully the LGBTQ community.

On June 28, 1969, police officers invaded the Stonewall Inn. But people there were fed up with the way they were being treated, so they stood their ground.

Word quickly spread. For several days, fighting took place at the Stonewall Inn as thousands of people joined in to help support the LGBTQ community.

This uprising became known as the Stonewall Riots.

The Stonewall Riots were an important turning point in the history of LGBTQ people. They began to openly voice their opinions and fight for equal rights. They formed LGBTQ advocacy groups, published newspapers, and organized parades and marches.

In 2009, President Barack Obama declared June "LGBT Pride Month." He said the Stonewall Riots were a reason to "commit to achieving equal justice under law for LGBT Americans."

We look back on those who took a stand at the Stonewall Riots as heroes who should be celebrated for giving LGBTQ people, like me, the freedoms we enjoy today.

One of these heroes was

Marsha P. Johnson

She was an African American drag artist, model, and LGBTQ activist.

Marsha was born Malcolm Michaels, Jr., on August 24, 1945, in New Jersey. She enjoyed wearing dresses starting at age five, but her family had difficulty accepting her for who she was. Marsha moved to New York City on her own after high school.

Although Marsha was often homeless and struggling, she was known for being bold, outspoken, and optimistic. When asked what the "P" in her name stood for, she would always reply, "Pay it no mind."

Marsha's goal was "to see gay people liberated and free and to have equal rights that other people have in America."

Marsha's friend

Sylvia Rivera,

a Latin American transgender activist, was another hero of the Stonewall Riots.

Sylvia was born Ray Rivera on July 2, 1951, in New York City. From a young age Sylvia knew she was transgender. Even though she looked like a boy, she felt like a girl inside. At age eleven, Sylvia ran away from home and was taken in by the local drag community.

In 1970, Sylvia and Marsha P. Johnson helped found STAR (Street Transgender Action Revolutionaries), one of the first organizations to help homeless transgender youth. Sylvia once said, "We have to be visible. We should not be ashamed of who we are. We have to show the world that we are numerous. There are many of us out there."

POLICE LINE

Today, Sylvia's legacy carries on. The Sylvia Rivera Law Project is an organization dedicated to assisting, supporting, training, and providing legal services for transgender and gender nonconforming people of color.

On June 28, 1970, the Christopher Street Liberation Day March was held in New York City to commemorate the one-year anniversary of the Stonewall Riots. It was the first LGBTQ Pride event in the United States.

Thousands of people gathered together and marched uptown on Sixth Avenue, ending with a "Gay-In" in Central Park's Sheep Meadow.

The official slogan for the event became "Pride." L. Craig Schoonmaker, a member of the march's planning committee, said, "A lot of people were very repressed, they were conflicted internally, and didn't know how to come out and be proud. That's how the movement was most useful, because they thought, *Maybe I should be proud.*'"

Soon marches were being held in other cities in the United States. Today, Pride is celebrated worldwide.

CHRISTOPHER STREET -19

In June 2015, I attended New York City's Pride March for the first time.

I took my time choosing the perfect outfit to wear that would express my personality.

I was overjoyed and enthusiastic when I arrived at the march. My parents were sure I would only walk a few blocks and want to quit. But I proved them wrong and danced the *entire* march route! I loved hearing people cheer. There were many smiles and even some happy tears.

The next day, I awoke to find out that I had become a *viral drag sensation.*

I have been dressing up in skirts, dresses, and tutus ever since I first discovered drag by watching the television show *RuPaul's Drag Race*. I thought RuPaul and the contestants were so beautiful and amazing, just like princesses. I said,

"I WANT TO DO THAT!"

My parents allowed me to explore dressing up and creating colorful characters, just like RuPaul.

RuPaul Andre Charles

was born on November 17, 1960, in California. He is a drag artist, actor, singer, songwriter, model, and host of several drag-themed television shows.

In 2009, RuPaul began producing the television show *RuPaul's Drag Race*, where drag artists compete in wacky challenges to be crowned the "Next Drag Superstar."

Unlike Sylvia Rivera, a transgender woman, RuPaul is a man who enjoys dressing up as a character in drag. It doesn't necessarily mean that he is transgender, although transgender people can also enjoy doing drag. *Anyone* can do drag!

RuPaul has brought the art of drag and LGBTQ culture into the mainstream. He has broken boundaries of what drag looks like and what drag artists can do with their performances.

I can freely be the character Desmond is Amazing because of the hard work of generations of people in the LGBTQ community.

Pepper LaBeija

Laverne Cox

James Baldwin

But there is still work to be done. The next generation of LGBTQ advocates, like me, are ready to continue to fight for our rights, strive for equality, and promote acceptance.

Miss Major

willi ninja

Stormé DeLarverie

Whether you love drag, like I do, or sports or science or art or computers or reading or math or something else no one's even heard of, *everyone* should be free to feel amazing, always.

What makes YOU amazing?

Pride is a feeling of honor and self-respect. It is the feeling of being worthwhile. It is having self-esteem.

We can all feel pride by expressing ourselves in a way that makes us happy or makes us feel beautiful, or in a way that feels right in our hearts. Simply put, self-expression is the art of being yourself, always.

Self-expression has no limits. You can be who you are no matter your age, race, orientation, identity, gender, financial status, class, disabilities, or abilities. You can like rap music or pop music. You can have long hair or short hair. You can wear dresses or shorts. There is no right or wrong way to be yourself.

Bullies are people who try to make you feel bad about yourself so they can feel better about themselves. They may say things like "You're queer," "You're a sissy," or "That's so gay." Using these terms as a way to insult others is never okay. Sometimes people will bully you when you are being yourself. That doesn't mean that there is something wrong with you. If you are getting bullied, or you see someone else getting bullied, tell an adult whom you trust.

You are beautiful, strong, and full of courage. Bullies will never be as fierce as you are. I follow the advice of Marsha P. Johnson. She said, "Pay it no mind. It's their issues not mine." I want you to remember to never let bullies hurt you. Just do you.

I want each and every one of you to express yourself today any way you want to. Today is YOUR pride!

With love,
Desmond is Amazing

Terms

The acronym "LGBTQ" stands for lesbian, gay, bisexual, transgender, and queer.

Everyone is different and unique. Some people have relationships with people of their own gender and some people have relationships with people of a different gender than the one they identify with.

Lesbian is a term used to describe a woman who is attracted to other women.

Gay is a term used to describe a man who is attracted to other men.

Bisexual is a term used to describe a person who is attracted to both men and women.

Transgender is a term used to describe people whose gender identity (or gender expression) is different than the gender they were assigned at birth.

Queer is an umbrella term used to describe a variety of gender identities. Sometimes the "Q" in LGBTQ can also stand for "questioning." **Questioning** is a term used to describe individuals who are still exploring their gender identity.

Gender nonconforming is a term used to describe someone who doesn't correspond to gender expectations in the way that they dress, act, or show interest in certain activities.

Gender fluid is a term used to describe a person whose gender identity is not fixed.

Sources

Barack Obama (2009). *Lesbian, Gay, Bisexual, and Transgender Pride Month, 2009.*
    Available at: https://web.archive.org/web/20100113194441/https://www.whitehouse.gov/
    the_press_office/Presidential-Proclamation-LGBT-Pride-Month. Accessed May 14, 2019.

Holland, Bryan. "How Activists Plotted the First Gay Pride Parades." Accessed May 14, 2019.
    https://www.history.com/news/how-activists-plotted-the-first-gay-pride-parades.

Romesburg, Don, ed. *The Routledge History of Queer America.* Routledge: New York, 2018.

Whose Streets Our Streets. "STAR House LES, 1970s." Accessed May 14, 2019. http://whose-
    streetsourstreets.org/star-house-les-1970s/.